Balance.

The Quick and Easy Guide to Achieving Financial Stability By Using a Budget

Dr. Jason L. Cabler

Text copyright © 2012 Dr. Jason L. Cabler

All Rights Reserved

Prologue

"The plan of the diligent leads surely to plenty, but those of everyone who is hasty, surely to poverty" Proverbs 21:5

I am firmly convinced that, if you want to be 100% sure that you succeed with money, you first have to know where all the money is going. If you just aren't sure where all your money goes every month and more times than not there is more month than money, this book is for you.

"**Balance…**" is a short book but its effect is very powerful in that the knowledge and practices you learn here will start you down the road toward greater financial prosperity.

A budget is simply a plan that takes you forward financially, not a look back at where everything went, and hoping you do better next time.

A plan for your money every month allows you to be proactive instead of reactive. It allows you to gain control where there has been a lack of control, and best of all, it brings you hope.

A consistent plan for your money brings you hope, because as you start to gain control of your situation, you begin to realize that you *actually can* have power and control over your financial life like you may have never had before.

Obviously making a budget is not sexy and it's not something most people aspire to do with their free time. But in order to truly gain control of your money, a budget *is* necessary. However, having the discipline to do one consistently every month can help you get out from under the financial stress that comes with not having full control, and that my friends is a great and wonderful thing!

Contents

Intro

Questions and Concerns
- What is a Monthly Spending Plan?
- Why Do I Need a Monthly Spending Plan?
- But I'm Scared...Why?
- What Does It Do For Me?
- How Do I Get Started?

The Plan
- Directions
- Monthly Spending Plan (Example p.1)
- What If I Have a Variable Income?
- Ok, Now You Completely Understand it, Right?

More Questions
- What if I Have No Idea What I Normally Spend on a Particular Category?
- What About Surprise Expenses?
- What Happens After I Fill Out My Plan?
- What Do I Do With the Cash I Need During the Month?
- What if an Envelope is Emptied Before the End of the Month?
- What if I Don't Want to Use the Envelope System?
- What If the Money in the Monthly Budget is Just Not Enough?
- So What Do I Do Now?

Spread the Word

About the Author

Intro

Celebrating Financial Freedom is not just a blog or a personal finance course; it's a way of life. It's all about learning how to become debt free and live a debt free lifestyle using solid Christian and common sense principles.

Learning to put together a workable monthly budget that makes sense is only a beginning step in taking control of your finances.

If you want even more great information on how to achieve debt freedom, I encourage you to begin reading articles on the CFF blog on a regular basis, and when you do that you'll discover that freedom from debt actually *is* achievable and that *anyone*, regardless of income, (yes, even you!) can unlock the shackles that have been keeping you enslaved to debt.

To receive weekly email updates from Celebrating Financial Freedom (No spam, I promise!) go to this link and sign up: **http://eepurl.com/e_zXY**

You can find the Celebrating Financial Freedom blog at **www.CFinancialFreedom.com**

When you finally realize that debt freedom actually *can* be a way of life for you and your family, your perspective suddenly changes. You start to realize that financial freedom is about much more than money:

- It's about having the freedom to make the best choices for your life because you don't have to consider your debt situation first.
- It's about living your most authentic life because debt freedom enables you to begin living the way *you* want to live and more easily pursue the best life that God has for you.
- It's about changing your family tree and leaving a lasting legacy. When you begin living these principles you become an example not only to your family, but to the world around you, leaving a lasting effect.

These are the things that Celebrating Financial Freedom is all about, and when you decide to become a regular reader and active participant, your perspective about money **will** change. You'll discover that how you use your money affects every single aspect of your life, for better or worse, and the wiser you are with it, the better your life will become.

Within these pages you will learn how to put together your own customized monthly spending plan (yes, a budget) so you can start taking control of how you use your money every single month and begin living a new and better financial life starting TODAY!

Questions and Concerns

 First off, I know you probably have some questions and concerns when it comes to starting up with a Monthly Spending Plan, so let's get those addressed right now.

What is a Monthly Spending Plan? Easy. A Monthly Spending Plan is what most people refer to as a "budget". Yes, I know that is a dirty word for most people, but guess what? Most people are broke. Why are most people broke? It's because they don't make any effort to make a consistent plan for their money. When you have a regular plan and you stick to it, you automatically start the process of having some financial discipline in your life, and you start the process of winning with money. It's that simple.

Why Do I Need a Monthly Spending Plan? You need a spending plan because if you're like most people, you have no idea where all your money goes and you let a lot of it just leak away because you don't have complete control over it.

A Monthly Spending Plan allows you to find out where those leaks are and plug them up, so those leaks don't eventually become a flood. When you're able to exercise control over your money, then it won't exercise control over you.

But I'm Scared...Why? When most people hear the word "budget" they don't like it, it sends shivers up their spine. When most people think of that word they think of restriction, deprivation, and suffering. The word "budget" to most people means they can't have any more fun or freedom, it's time to buckle down and eat ramen noodles and cut off the cable TV.

 But a monthly spending plan is not about that at all. It's about freeing yourself from the tyranny of wondering where it all went when there's more month left than there is money. It's about the freedom of knowing how much you have to spend and not adding to your stressful debt load because what's going out is equal to what's coming in.

It's about gaining control of your situation and changing your life for the better because you decided it was time to quit fooling around and start succeeding with your money.

Yes, change is scary and sometimes hard, but it's rarely as hard as you think it's going to be, and it's always worth it in the end.

When it comes down to it, this is the kind of change that will make your life better in the long run. It will give you freedom and hope, and that's a good deal.

What Does It Do For Me? A Monthly Spending Plan allows you to put a name on every dollar so you can use your money as efficiently as possible and eliminate waste due to the little money leaks that easily go unnoticed and can really add up over time.

A Monthly Spending Plan is important for you to do every single month, and it's especially important if you're trying to get out of debt. You'll find that if you make a consistent effort and stick to it, you'll discover money you didn't know you had.

You'll be able to see where money is being wasted and you can eliminate that waste as you see fit by spending less in that area, or by putting it somewhere else (like into savings, paying down debt, or wherever else you'd like to put it).

Whether your situation is completely off the rails or it just needs a little tweaking, a Monthly Spending Plan helps you get back on track.

How Do I Get Started? The absolute first thing you have to do is *decide*. You have to decide that *now is the time* to do something different. Now is the time to take control and *become committed* to getting control of your money. Deciding to commit to the process and form new habits is the essential first step to having a successful plan.

Next, you have to be honest. Sit down with the monthly spending plan forms and fill them out to the best of your ability. Be as honest as possible, and remember, budgeting is a dirty process, it's never 100% perfect and you *will* have some difficulty at first because you may not have done much financial planning before (if at all).

YOU WILL NOT GET IT RIGHT THE FIRST TIME!!!

...or the second, or the third. But as you do it every month it will get easier, it will take less time, and it will make more sense to you. Eventually it will become second nature. I had the same difficulty when I started this stuff too. So **keep focused** and eventually it will make sense.

It's just like when I learned how to ride a bike. I was shaky and unconfident at first, but after a few months I was jumping ramps like Evel Knievel.

So now that I've addressed some initial concerns and questions, let's dive headfirst into the actual process of putting together a plan. Below you'll find directions on how to get started, as well as a sample Monthly Spending Plan that will give you a pretty good idea of how your plan might look once you put it together.

The Plan

The Monthly Spending Plan is a ZERO BASED spending plan, which means that you will spend every single dollar on paper before you spend it in real life. This is what helps you make sure that the money GOING OUT is equal to the money COMING IN.

There is a category in this plan for most anything you would spend money on in a normal month. Some of these categories you'll just leave blank because you don't normally spend money on these things.

The sample plan on the next three pages is based on a $5,000 monthly household TAKE HOME income. Your monthly take home income may be more or less and that's OK, this is just an example to get you started. This plan will work whether you make $100 or $100,000 a month.

***Download blank Monthly Spending Plan budgeting forms for printing using this link:
http://wp.me/P1yqwF-xn***

Directions

1. Scroll down to page 3 of the Sample Monthly Spending Plan. At the bottom of the page you will see entered a total monthly income ($5,000) in the "Grand Total" column.
2. Next, note the blanks filled in for each different category. If there is a category you don't use, you would leave it blank.
3. If you have a bill that you pay every six months or once a year (such as life insurance or car insurance) divide the yearly cost by 12 to get how much that bill will cost you each month. For example, if your life insurance is $120 per year, put $10 ($120 divided by 12 months) in the blank. You can keep that money as cash in an envelope or in a separate bank account used to pay that bill when it comes due.
4. When page one is finished being filled out, you add everything up and enter the total on the "page 1 totals" line.
5. Do the same for pages 2 and 3.
6. Once you have your total for each page, you will enter those totals at the bottom of page 3 and add them up to get a grand total. That grand total should be equal to the "total household income" you entered earlier on page 3.

As you can see in this example, the $5,000 grand total (which is the money going out) minus the $5,000 income (the money coming in) will equal ZERO. Why does it need to equal zero? So that you are NOT spending more than you make and so that every dollar has a place to go. When you know where every dollar is going you don't have to spend time wondering what happened to all of your money. Your money will begin ACTUALLY making sense to you.

Monthly Spending Plan (Example p.1)- Download blank forms using this link: http://wp.me/P1yqwF-xn

	Amount Budgeted	Total	Actually Spent
Charity			
Tithe	500		
Offering	25		
Other_____	_____	525	_____
Savings			
Emergency Fund	150		
Retirement (IRA, 401k, etc.)	_____		_____
College	_____	150	_____
Food			
Groceries	400		
Restaurants	75	475	
Utilities			
Home Phone	_____		_____
Cell Phones	100		
Cable	50		
Trash	25		
Electric	150		
Gas	75		
Water	40	440	
Housing			
House Payment/Rent	800		
Second Mortgage	_____		_____
Homeowner's Insurance	50		
Real Estate Taxes	50		
Furniture	_____		_____
Repairs	_____		_____
Maintenance Fees	_____		_____
Other_____	_____	900	_____
Medical/Dental			
Medicine	100		
Insurance	350		
Dentist Bill	70		
Doctor Bill	_____		_____
Eye Doctor	_____	520	_____
Page 1 Totals		3010	_____

Monthly Spending Plan (Example p.2)

Transportation	Amount Budgeted	Total	Actually Spent
Car Payment 1	350		
Car Payment2			
Fuel	420		
Car Insurance	100		
Repairs, Maint., Tires	100		
Car Replacement			
License, Fees, Taxes	30		
Bus, Cab, Train Fares		1000	
Insurances			
Life Insurance	25		
Disability Insurance			
Pet Health Insurance		25	
Clothing			
Adults	75		
Children	50	125	
Recreational			
Vacation			
Entertainment	50	50	
Educational			
Day Care			
School Tuition			
School Supplies	30	30	
Various			
Babysitter			
Child Support			
Alimony			
Club/Org. Dues			
Cosmetics	30		
Toiletries	30		
Gifts (Including Christmas)	75		
Subscriptions			
Hair Care	75		
Other_____			
Other_____			
Other_____			
Other_____			
Discretionary	100	310	
2nd Page Totals		1540	

Monthly Spending Plan (Example p.3)

Debt Reduction	Amount Budgeted	Total	Actually Spent
Student Loan 1	125		
Student Loan 2			
Finance Company 1			
Finance Company 2			
Credit Line 1	100		
Credit Line 2			
Mastercard 1	75		
Mastercard 2			
Visa 1			
Visa 2			
Discover Card 1	50		
Discover Card 2			
American Express 1			
American Express 2			
Dept. Store Card 1			
Dept. Store Card 2			
Gas Card 1			
Gas Card 2			
Family Member Loan 1	100		
Family Member Loan 2			
Other_____			
Other_____			
Other_____			
Other_____		450	
3rd Page Totals		450	
2nd Page Totals		1540	
1st Page Totals		3010	
Grand Total		5000	
Minus Total Household Income		5000	
	Equals	0	

What If I Have a Variable Income?

Not everybody has a consistent salary that doesn't vary from paycheck to paycheck. I certainly don't. My income can vary by as much as 50% from month to month, which, if you don't know how to budget for that, it can be a real nightmare.

For my situation (I get paid once per month), what works best is to use the zero based budgeting forms above that break all expenses down into various categories. Once I know how much my paycheck is, usually on the second day of the month, then I fill in my budget before spending even one penny of that money.

However, if you get paid weekly or biweekly, how you budget is only slightly more complicated, with only one additional step involved. You still need the usual budgeting forms just to look at the list of individual budget items for a reference.

Then you make a list by asking yourself this question: "If I only have enough money to pay for one line item in my budget, what would that be?" Obviously the most important things come first, such as shelter, food, water, electricity, etc.

Put the most important item at the top of the list and then ask the question again: "If I can only pay for one more thing, what is the next most important thing?", and so on until you run out of money from your paycheck.

As you work your way down the list, you subtract what you've spent until you get to zero.

Here's a Quick Demo to Get You Started:

Let's say you get paid every two weeks. Your latest paycheck is $2,000 and that money is supposed to pay your expenses for the next 2 weeks. Those expenses include everything from food and shelter to savings and giving.

You make a list with 3 columns labeled "Item", "Amount", and "Amount Left". (You can find premade forms to print using this link: **http://wp.me/P1yqwF-xn**)

So you start with $2,000 and the top item of importance is your house payment. Your monthly house payment is $800. So you enter "House Payment" as the first budget item under the "Item" column.

Then you enter $400 (which is ½ of your house payment, you'll pay the other half with your next paycheck) under the "Amount Column".

Then you enter $1,600 (which is $2,000 minus $400) under the "Amount Left" column.

You then work your way down your list of budgeted items in order of importance such as food, water, electricity, transportation, etc. until the "Amount Left" column equals zero. You now have the next two weeks of spending planned ahead of time, and when you stick to it, you won't spend more than you make.

It should look like this:

Item	Amount	Amount Left
House payment	$400	$1,600
Food	$250	$1,350

And so on...

When you get paid in two more weeks, you do the same process over again, planning the next two weeks expenses until you get to zero.

When you finally get to zero, you are done spending and you don't spend anything else. This helps ensure that you have a balanced budget and you don't end up spending more than you make. When all of the money in the budget is spent, do not, under any circumstance, whip out the credit cards! In fact, cut them up so you're not tempted.

Ok, Now You Completely Understand it, Right?

Of course I'm joking. At this point it's likely that you may be a little **Dazed** and **Confused**. I don't expect you to totally get it just yet. Like I said, it will take time. So take a deep breath and remember, the more you do it the more you'll get it.

Look over the sample Spending Plan again if you need to. Look over it several times and try and really see what's going on, don't just gloss over it quickly and say to yourself "I don't get this stuff".

If your eyes are glazing over after the first couple of times, then come back to it later. You might have to sit down with it a few times before it starts making some kind of sense to you. You'll see something different every time you look at it and eventually the pieces will start coming together. It might even be helpful to review the entire course 2-3 times to get a complete grasp of how all of this works.

The most important thing is to NOT GIVE UP. Just because you may not fully get it at first doesn't mean it's not doable. Just like learning to ride that bike, you may get a few bumps and scrapes at first, but you'll eventually get it.

More Questions

By now I'm sure you have a few more questions. So let's get those out of the way and I'll see if I can clear up a few things for you.

What if I Have No Idea What I Normally Spend on a Particular Category? Just estimate it as close as you can and write it in the blank. As you do it more you'll get a better feel for what you need in every particular category every month.

What About Surprise Expenses? Sometimes surprises can come up during the month that you just could not predict if you tried. But you can keep those surprises from *holding you hostage*. If you are sticking to the plan and putting money back for things like home repairs, car repairs, etc. these don't set you back because you have prepared for them in advance.

Still, things can come up that don't really fit into any category and are just plain unpredictable. What do you do about those? You plan for the unpredictable by putting some money into the "discretionary" category at the bottom of page 2, or you can write in "Surprise Expenses" in the blank beside one of the categories I've labeled as "Other" also at the end of page 2 on your budgeting forms.

What Happens After I Fill Out My Plan? Once you have your Monthly Spending Plan filled out, that is your blueprint for the month.

Now you can go ahead and start paying your bills and sending the money where it needs to go. Just remember to stick to the plan.

What Do I Do With the Cash I Need During the Month? Here's what I do: I add up all the categories for which I need cash during the month and I take it out of the bank. I then divvy it up into envelopes and spend money out of those envelopes. For example, my wife and I have envelopes for Gas, Groceries, Clothing, Eating Out, Entertainment, and several others.

Since we don't use credit cards this is what works best for us. If we use up all the money in a particular envelope before the month is over then we don't spend any more on that category.

That forces us to be aware of what we're spending so the money will last the entire month, but it also has the added effect of ensuring that we don't spend more than we make.

Learning to use this "Envelope Method" it might be a little strange at first using cash instead of whipping out a credit card. But eventually you'll get skilled at managing your cash to make it last the entire month instead of wondering how much you put on the credit card.

What if an Envelope is Emptied Before the End of the Month? If you get to the middle of the month and an envelope is empty, then one of two things probably happened. Either you budgeted too little or you spent too much.

At that point you need to be honest with yourself. You need to decide if that category is one where you need better self control, or did you just underestimate how much you needed?

If you have a family of four and you budgeted only $200 for groceries for the month, you need to put more in that category, your family needs to eat. But if you put $400 in your entertainment envelope and you burned through it in the first two weeks, then you may want to reevaluate your priorities and make some changes.

We've been using the envelope system for many years now and it works well for us, but sometimes we still run out of money in an envelope before the end of the month. If that happens, we don't spend any more on that category until next month.

However, sometimes we may pull money out of another envelope if we feel the need.

For instance, if we decide we want to go see a movie but the "entertainment" envelope has run dry, we may take some from the "Eating Out" envelope, and that's ok, we'll just be eating out less this month. We made the decision that today a movie is more important than a meal at a restaurant and we found a way to pay for it without using money we didn't have (i.e. credit cards)

But you can't get stupid with it. You DO NOT take money out of the "Gas" envelope to eat out or see a movie. You DO NOT take money out of the "Groceries" envelope to buy cute shoes or go play a round of golf. Those are necessities you shouldn't be messing around with.

What if I Don't Want to Use the Envelope System? There are other ways you can keep up with your spending categories without stuffing envelopes with cash.

You can open an account with ING Direct or Ally Bank. These are web based banks that offer accounts that are highly customizable. You can set up an account with as many subcategories as you like and allocate money to those categories just like you would fill an envelope.

Every time you make a purchase with your debit card, you go online through a smartphone app or computer and designate which category your purchase was from, and the money is taken out of that category, sort of like using a virtual envelope system.

There are also smartphone apps out there that do the same thing but are not tied to any particular bank (Mint.com is the most popular one). You just set up your accounts with your spending categories on their secure site and it works the same as the banking sites mentioned above.

What If the Money in the Monthly Budget is Just Not Enough? If you put your budget together and you feel like you just don't have enough money in there to make it for the entire month, you probably have one of two common problems. Either you're spending too much, or you're not making enough to cover your basic expenses.

The first thing you do is to break out the chainsaw and cut out all unnecessary expenses. Now is the time you will have to be ruthless and sacrificial, because continuing to increase debt is not an option. You may need to reduce or get rid of your cable TV plan, stop eating out, or even find a cheaper car or place to live, among other things.

If you've cut everything to the bone and still don't have enough, it's time to get start getting really honest with yourself and realize that you just may not be making enough to totally support even your basic needs. You'll need to consider finding ways to increase your income.

Fortunately, now more than ever before, there are tons of ways to do that that weren't available just over a decade ago. You can read the following posts from my blog to start getting some ideas.

"5 Ways to Make Extra Money, Even in a Tough Economy" at this link:

http://wp.me/p1yqwF-fS

"Another 5 Ways to Make Extra Money, Even in a Tough Economy" at this link:

http://wp.me/p1yqwF-iS

So What Do I Do Now? Now is the time to get started putting together your own plan. On the following pages you will find blank Monthly Spending Plan pages for you to fill out on your own. You will need to print them off (make sure to print only pages 26, 27, 28) and use a pencil to fill out the sheets (so you can erase as needed). I recommend printing out multiple copies so you will have enough forms handy for the next few months. That way you don't have the psychological barrier of having to start up the computer, open the file, and print out new forms every time.

Remember, this is about forming new habits, so the fewer barriers in your way the better.

Ok, it's time to get down to business and fill out your own customized plan. Remember, you won't get it right the first few months and it's never 100% perfect. So take a deep breath, don't stress, and just do it. You'll get the hang of it.

If you have any questions or just can't figure something out with this whole Monthly Spending Plan thing, feel free to email me at:

jasoncabler@cfinancialfreedom.com

If you are reading this on a format such as a Kindle, Nook, IPad, or other e-reader, you can use your computer to download the forms for printing using this link:

http://wp.me/P1yqwF-xn

Spread the Word

I just want to take the time to thank you and tell you how much I appreciate the role you are playing in my goal to change people's financial lives for the better.

If you found this Monthly Spending Plan helpful to you, please make sure to pay it forward and recommend it to someone who you think can benefit from it. The whole point of this Book is to change lives, and by spreading the word, you can have a part in that.

By telling others about this book, you will motivate me tremendously by encouraging me to produce similar helpful material in the future, and more importantly you will help change the lives of countless people like you who desperately want to change their financial situation for the better and begin succeeding financially.

Please don't forget to also tell your friends about my Celebrating Financial Freedom website and blog. You can also connect with and follow me on Facebook, Twitter, Google+, and Pinterest and opt in to twice weekly emails (no spam, I promise!)

Opt in to Emails: http://eepurl.com/e_zXY

Blog: www.CFinancialFreedom.com

Twitter: www.twitter.com/drcabler

Facebook: www.facebook.com/celebratingfinancialfreedom

Pinterest: www.pinterest.com/jasoncabler

Google+: www.plus.google.com/jasoncabler

Monthly Spending Plan Forms (Blank) Find printable forms at this link:
http://wp.me/P1yqwF-xn

Monthly Spending Plan (page 1)

	Budgeted Amount	Total	Actually Spent
Charity			
Tithe	_____		_____
Offering	_____		_____
Other_____	_____	_____	_____
Savings			
Emergency Fund	_____		_____
Retirement (IRA, 401k, etc.)	_____		_____
College	_____	_____	_____
Food			
Groceries	_____		_____
Restaurants	_____	_____	_____
Utilities			
Home Phone	_____		_____
Cell Phone	_____		_____
Cable	_____		_____
Trash	_____		_____
Electric	_____		_____
Gas	_____		_____
Water	_____	_____	_____
Housing			
House Payment	_____		_____
Second Mortgage	_____		_____
Homeowner's Insurance	_____		_____
Real Estate Taxes	_____		_____
Furniture	_____		_____
Repairs	_____		_____
Maintenance Fees	_____		_____
Other_____	_____	_____	_____
Medical/Dental			
Medicine	_____		_____
Insurance	_____		_____
Dentist Bill	_____		_____
Doctor Bill	_____		_____
Eye Doctor	_____	_____	_____
Page 1 Totals	_____	_____	_____

Monthly Spending Plan (p.2)

Category	Amount Budgeted	Total	Actually Spent
Transportation			
Car Payment 1	_____		_____
Car Payment 2	_____		_____
Fuel	_____		_____
Car Insurance	_____		_____
Repairs, Maint., Tires	_____		_____
Car Replacement	_____		_____
License, Fees, Taxes	_____		_____
Bus, Cab, Train Fares	_____	_____	_____
Insurances			
Life Insurance	_____		_____
Disability Insurance	_____		_____
Pet Health Insurance	_____	_____	_____
Clothing			
Adults	_____		_____
Children	_____	_____	_____
Recreational			
Vacation	_____		_____
Entertainment	_____	_____	_____
Educational			
Day Care	_____		_____
School Tuition	_____		_____
School Supplies	_____	_____	_____
Various			
Babysitter	_____		_____
Child Support	_____		_____
Alimony	_____		_____
Club/Org. Dues	_____		_____
Cosmetics	_____		_____
Toiletries	_____		_____
Gifts (Including Christmas)	_____		_____
Subscriptions	_____		_____
Hair Care	_____		_____
Other_____	_____		_____
Other_____	_____		_____
Other_____	_____		_____
Other_____	_____		_____
Discretionary	_____	_____	_____
2nd Page Totals	_____	_____	_____

Monthly Spending Plan (p.3)

Debt Reduction	Amount Budgeted	Total	Actually Spent
Student Loan 1	_____		_____
Student Loan 2	_____		_____
Finance Company 1	_____		_____
Finance Company 2	_____		_____
Credit Line 1	_____		_____
Credit Line 2	_____		_____
Mastercard 1	_____		_____
Mastercard 2	_____		_____
Visa 1	_____		_____
Visa 2	_____		_____
Discover Card 1	_____		_____
Discover Card 2	_____		_____
American Express 1	_____		_____
American Express 2	_____		_____
Dept. Store Card 1	_____		_____
Dept. Store Card 2	_____		_____
Gas Card 1	_____		_____
Gas Card 2	_____		_____
Family Member Loan 1	_____		_____
Family Member Loan 2	_____		_____
Other_____	_____		_____
Other_____	_____		_____
Other_____	_____		_____
Other_____	_____	_____	_____

3rd Page Totals   _____   _____   _____

2nd Page Totals   _____   _____   _____

1st Page Totals   _____   _____   _____

Grand Total   _____   _____

Total Household Income   _____
                                                                        0

Monthly Spending Plan: Variable Income (Blank)   Find printable forms at this link: http://wp.me/P1yqwF-xn

Item	Amount	Amount Left
_____	_____	_____
_____	_____	_____
_____	_____	_____
_____	_____	_____
_____	_____	_____
_____	_____	_____
_____	_____	_____
_____	_____	_____
_____	_____	_____
_____	_____	_____
_____	_____	_____
_____	_____	_____
_____	_____	_____

About the Author

I'm Dr. Jason Cabler, and I've been reading about, writing about, and teaching Christian personal finance for the better part of a decade now. In the early part of our marriage, my wife Angie and I were in debt, and we found that that debt was a constant drag on our finances, our relationship, and on our happiness in general.

When we finally decided to do something about it we took a popular "get out of debt" course where our perspectives about money started to change. We began to come together as one financially, and to my surprise, in the middle of one session Angie unexpectedly cut up every single credit card we had in front of the entire group! Our journey to debt freedom had begun.

Opt in to Email Updates at this link: **http://eepurl.com/e_zXY**

Opt in to RSS feed at this link: **http://feeds.feedburner.com/cfinancialfreedom/QtGy**

But even though we were starting to think alike financially, we didn't fully commit to the process and fell back into some old habits that kept us from getting free from our debt and truly succeeding financially.

After another year or two of having those nagging debts cause stress in our marriage, we finally decided to fully commit to the process and made a written plan to get out of debt and began putting together a written budget every single month, and that made all the difference.

We finally began working with a plan instead of flying by the seat of our pants.

We finally made a commitment to each other to never finance another car, open another credit card, or use any kind of credit whatsoever, and that is the moment when we began succeeding with money!

Even though the bad economy has taken a toll on my income, we have since become debt free except for our house, paid cash for a luxury car, and can't remember the last time we had an argument about money!

During this process I became extremely passionate about personal finance and how it can truly change lives for the better. I began reading every book on the subject and eventually developed my own course that I now teach live and have also made available as a self study course with a workbook and 4 audio cd's.

My Celebrating Financial Freedom course will not only teach you how to get out of debt using simple Christian and common sense principles, it will teach you how to communicate better with your spouse, how to keep from making stupid mistakes with money, and how using your money wisely not only affects you, but the rest of the world around you, for better or for worse.

So if you are at that point in your life where you know it's time to learn more about getting out of debt, and better yet, take action to get out of debt, then consider purchasing the Celebrating Financial Freedom course. You will not regret it. The course is available at this link: **http://wp.me/P1yqwF-13**

If you have any questions about the course or anything else dealing with personal finance, please feel free to email me at **jasoncabler@cfinancialfreedom.com** and I'll be glad to answer any questions you may have.

www.ingramcontent.com/pod-product-compliance
Lightning Source LLC
Chambersburg PA
CBHW070734180526
45167CB00004B/1752